Feeling **Wronged** &
Learning *Forgiveness*™

Liam Conquers Fort Grudge™

SOPHIA DAY®

KEEP OUT!

WELCOME

D1249402

Written by Megan Johnson   *Illustrated by* Stephanie Strouse

The Sophia Day® Creative Team-
Megan Johnson, Stephanie Strouse,
Kayla Pearson, Timothy Zowada, Celestte Dills, Mel Sauder

A **special thank you** to our team of reviewers who graciously gives us feedback, edits, and help ensure that our products remain accurate, applicable, and genuinely diverse.

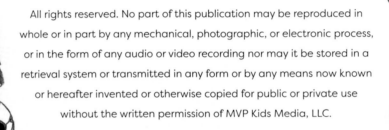

Published and Distributed by MVP Kids Media, LLC -
Mesa, Arizona, USA
Printed by Prosperous Printing Inc. -
Shenzhen, China

Designed by Stephanie Strouse

DOM Mar 2020, Job # 02-011-01

May your childhood be filled with adventure, your days with hope, and your learnings with wisdom, and may you continuously grow as an MVP Kid, preparing to lead a responsible, meaningful life.

-SOPHIA DAY

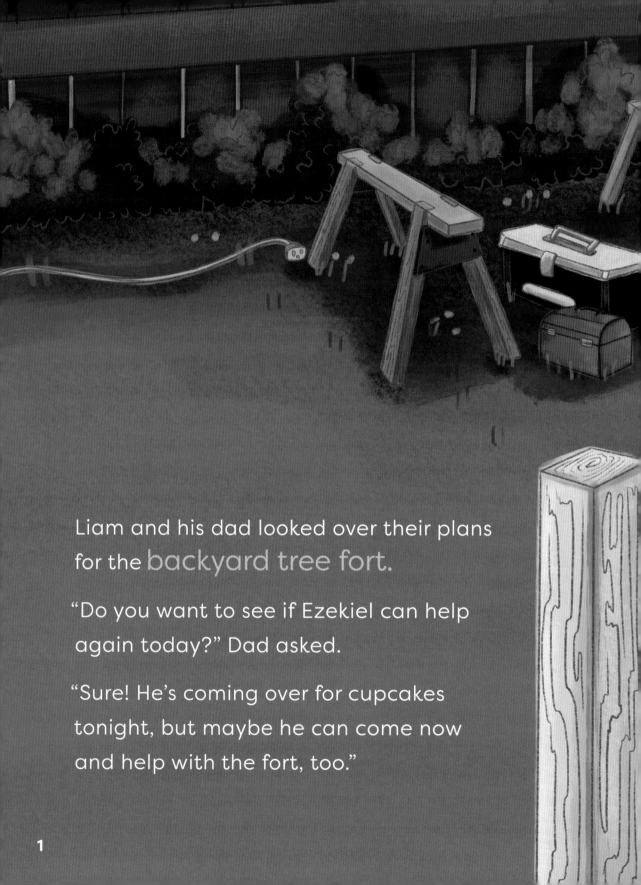

Liam and his dad looked over their plans for the backyard tree fort.

"Do you want to see if Ezekiel can help again today?" Dad asked.

"Sure! He's coming over for cupcakes tonight, but maybe he can come now and help with the fort, too."

2

Liam borrowed his dad's phone
and sent Ezekiel a message.

3

4

"Ezekiel has plans. Let's get started," said Liam.

"Okay. You measure the lengths, and I'll cut the boards, then you can do the sanding."

When all of the boards had been cut, sanded, and sorted, they were ready to finish the house and add the railing.

"Oops. Looks like we need more nails," Dad said.

"I'll ride to the store with you," offered Liam's older sister, Esme.

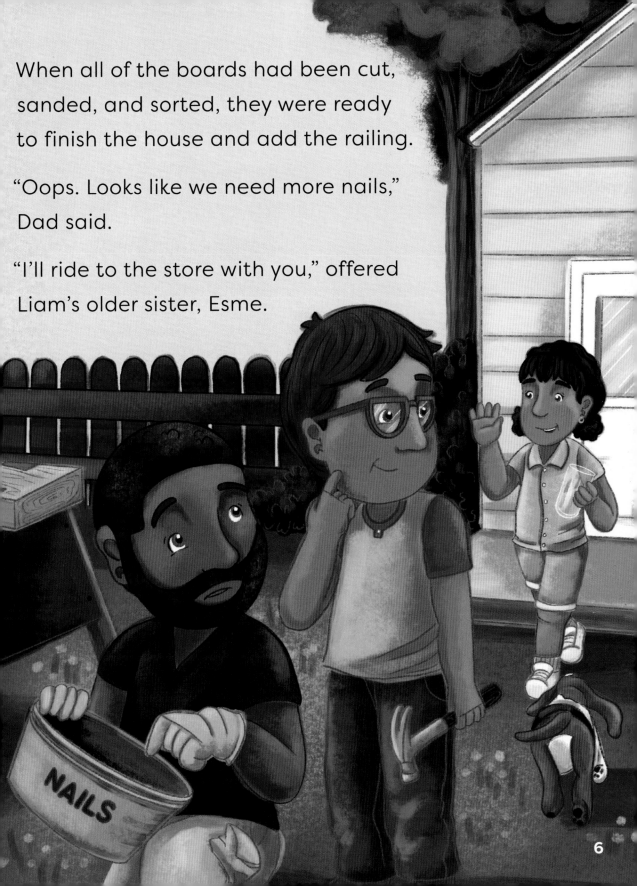

Liam and Esme rode their bikes to the hobby store around the corner. As they passed Ezekiel's house, Liam glanced at the family car.

That's funny, he thought. *Ezekiel said they had plans, but it looks like they're home.*

Liam found the nails he needed, and Esme picked out some paint.

"Working on your fort, I see," said Mr. Frank. "I'm surprised you're not at Ezekiel's."

"He had plans today, or he'd be helping us."

"But I thought—never mind. How is the fort coming along?"

"I think we'll finish it today," Liam said proudly.

"Well, you enjoy that fort with your friends."

"Thanks, Mr. Frank. See you next time!"

On his way home, Liam noticed a lot of activity at Ezekiel's house.

It looks like he did have plans—BIG plans.
And I thought we were friends.

Back at home, Liam was lost in thought while passing the boards up to his dad.

Maybe it wasn't what it looked like.

No, it was definitely a party. I'm sure of it!

Liam hoped that building would distract him from his angry thoughts. Instead, his thoughts distracted him from building.

He's so mean. He must not like me.

We weren't that good of friends, anyway.

"OUCH!" he whacked his thumb with the hammer.

"You were hitting those nails pretty hard. Are you okay?"

Liam told his dad what he saw on his bike ride.

"I'm sure there's an explanation. We'll figure it out when he comes over tonight," said Dad.

"He's NOT coming over tonight," answered Liam firmly.

If Ezekiel doesn't want me at his party, I don't want him in my fort, he thought.

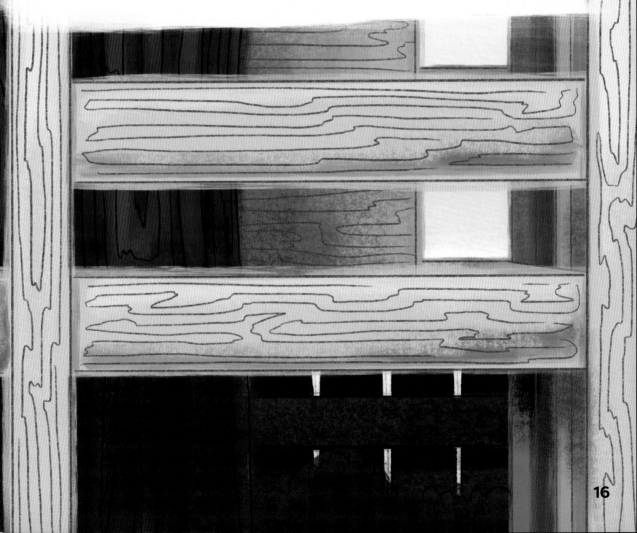

They finished the house and railings. Aside from the extra dings from Liam's hammer, it was looking just like their plans.

"Time to build the ladder," Dad said.

"Actually, I was thinking we should make a rope ladder," said Liam.

"But we need the rope for your communication line into Ezekiel's yard."

"I changed my mind. I want the rope ladder instead."

So, they cut the rope and drilled holes into the ladder rungs. Liam tied a strong knot under each board.

18

"There's just enough wood left for the welcome sign, and here is some chain for hanging it," Liam's dad said.

"But we have some extra hinges. I'd rather make a door that closes when the ladder is up."

Liam measured the hole and helped his dad cut the pieces to make his fortress secure.

"You know, Liam, shutting out your friend won't make you feel better. Holding a grudge* only hurts yourself."

*__Holding a grudge__ means living with anger when someone hurts or offends you.

21

Liam started bringing up the items he planned to have in his fort—comics, toys, and games to play with his friends. He tried to enjoy it, but he only felt anger and sadness.

This really would be more fun with my friends, he thought.

Liam was happy to be distracted by dinner. He listened with more attention than usual as his mom described her day at work.

"...And then I got home in time to finish the cupcakes for Ezekiel's birthday!" she said.

Ezekiel's cupcakes! Oh no! He had forgotten that Ezekiel was coming over after dinner.

"You'll have to call his mom and tell him not to come. I don't want to see him today. He had a birthday party and didn't even invite me! He's not my friend anymore."

"You can't just avoid him. If you don't work it out, you're holding a grudge, and holding a grudge—"

"Only hurts myself," Liam finished with a sigh.

Liam was upset at his mom now, too. *Why won't she just back me up on this?* he thought. *Why does she have to be on his side?*

Liam climbed the ladder, pulled it up, and closed the trap door. He wrote "keep out" on a piece of cardboard and posted it on the railing.

Ezekiel deserves to feel left out, too, he thought.

Then, he went inside the tree house and closed the door just in time to hear his mom's voice saying, "I don't see him, but I'm sure he's up there."

"Liam?" Ezekiel looked around the tree
trunk for the ladder, but couldn't find it.
"Um, remember we had plans for cupcakes?"

Ezekiel paused, waiting for a response.

"Okay, then. Another time, I guess." He left disappointed.

28

The next day, Liam was in his fort when he heard neighborhood kids riding bikes in the street.

"Hi, guys! How's it going?" he shouted.

"Hi, Liam! *Wow!* Your fort looks great!" said Leo.

"We're setting up some street races. Want to come?" asked Olivia.

"Sure! I'll be right down."

Just then, he heard another voice in the street.

"Hi, guys! I'll race, too!"
It was Ezekiel.

"Great!"
said Olivia.
"We'll get started
as soon as Liam
comes."

Liam wasn't ready to
hang out with Ezekiel yet.
He climbed back up the ladder,
and locked the hatch again.

Meanwhile, his friends were waiting on him.

"Ezekiel, go ring his doorbell and see if he's coming."

"Nah, he'll come if he wants to come. Let's just play."

"What's going on?" asked Olivia. "I thought you guys were friends."

"I thought so, too, but maybe we're not."

34

Olivia could tell from his tone that she should drop it, but her sister Marie had her own way of keeping peace. "Friends!" she declared as she grabbed Ezekiel's hand and led him to Liam's door.

Mrs. Johnson answered. "Hi! I'm so glad you came. Liam is up in the fort."

"I don't know if he wants to see me," Ezekiel said.

"Well, let's go find out."

"Liam, please let us in. Ezekiel wants to talk."

"I don't feel like talking," Liam answered.

"All of your friends are outside waiting for you. You think this fort—this grudge—is protecting you, but it is isolating you instead."

His mom was right.

What good was this fort
if he couldn't share it
with his friends?

It was scary to open up the door. What if he and Ezekiel couldn't make up?

39

He had to take the risk.
Feeling alone
was miserable.

"I'm sorry about the party. It was just with school friends. I didn't think you'd have much fun not knowing anyone," Ezekiel said.

"I forgive you. I'm sorry, too. I should have just talked to you about it instead of shutting you out."

"Friends?"
Liam asked.

"Forever,"
Ezekiel agreed.

"Hey, guys! Change of plans!" shouted Liam. "Come help me finish our fort!"

The friends worked together to make a true friendship FORT, built on...

Forgiveness—letting go of the pain and anger someone caused, and wishing good instead of revenge.

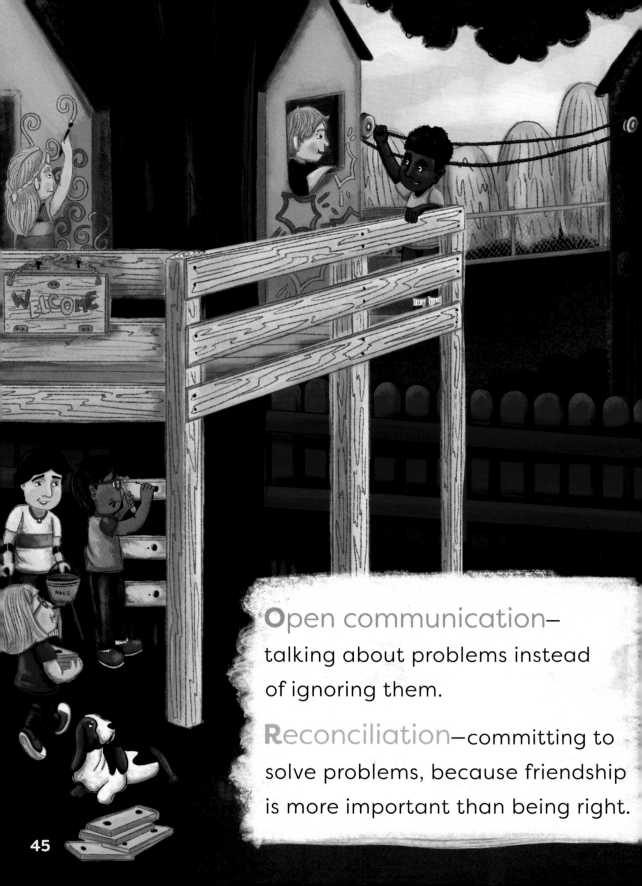

Open communication–
talking about problems instead
of ignoring them.

Reconciliation–committing to
solve problems, because friendship
is more important than being right.

Trust—choosing to be dependable, and believing the other person will be there for you, too.

Sometimes a friend will let you down,
Hurt your feelings, do you wrong.
You might think, *She's not my friend.*
He's been mean all along.

Friendships are important,
So do not rush to judge.
You only heap hurt on yourself
When you hold on to a grudge.

Forgiveness means you're letting go
Of what you're mad about.
Instead of wishing for revenge,
Try to work it out.

Openly communicate;
Say what's bothering you.
Apologize for any ways
You may have caused hurt, too.

Reconcile, stop arguing,
and work to get along.
Trust will rebuild. Over time,
Your friendship will be strong.

LEARN & DISCUSS

Liam is learning to understand grudges and practicing how to forgive. Learn with Liam and discover how you can forgive a friend when you have been wronged, too.

There's nothing wrong with feeling hurt or angry. That's a natural response when someone offends you. Being hurt by Ezekiel's party shows how much I care about our friendship.

Think about the last time you were hurt by someone else. What happened?

What does your hurt show you about your relationship with that person?

Holding a grudge means to choose to stay angry, hoping that holding back your forgiveness and friendship will hurt the other person, too.

What are some signs that I was holding a grudge against Ezekiel?

Are you holding a grudge? Ask yourself these questions to find out.
  - *Are you still angry about something that happened in the past?*
  - *Are you avoiding the person who upset you?*
  - *Do you think you can get revenge by staying angry?*

If you answered yes to those questions, you are probably holding a grudge. Holding on to your hurt might feel like the best thing to do for a little while, but it actually becomes more painful to you the longer you stay upset. Holding a grudge does not only hurt the other person; it hurts you.

What did I miss out on because I was holding a grudge against my friend? Did this hurt Ezekiel or me?

Think about a grudge or a hurt that you hold on to. How does that grudge have the power to keep hurting you?

People often have the wrong idea about forgiveness.
Here are some things forgiveness is **NOT**:
- Requiring that the offender proves to be sorry
- Accepting someone's excuse for hurting you
- Saying, "it's not a big deal" when it really was a big deal
- Continuing a relationship that is unhealthy

Describe what you think forgiveness means.

Forgiveness is all up to you! It's your own decision to let go of a hurt and decide not to let it control your feelings or actions anymore. You can choose not to feel angry toward the person who hurt you. You can wish for good to happen to that person rather than for revenge. After you forgive, it is up to you whether you want to continue the relationship, but the important thing is that you have no more hard feelings.

When is it most difficult for you to forgive?

Is it possible to forgive someone who hasn't apologized? Why or why not?

Is it possible to forgive someone and also end the friendship? Why or why not?

Forgiveness isn't about being right; it's about making a relationship right. When you've been hurt, communicate openly, and don't make people guess at how they hurt you. Sometimes, like with Ezekiel, it is unintentional or even out of the other person's control. If you want to stop being isolated by your grudge, do what I did, and rebuild your friendship FORT with the four steps below.

Forgiveness – *Stop letting the hurt control you. Choose to treat the other person well.*

Open Communication – *Tell your friend how you were offended and give them a chance to explain. Apologize for any wrong you're responsible for in the situation.*

Reconciliation – *Express that you want your friendship to continue. Focus on what you have in common.*

Trust – *Rebuild your trust in each other. This may take time.*

Help your child understand holding grudges and choosing forgiveness.

Acknowledge imperfection. Children often idealize others and become especially upset when let down by a good friend or a role model. Help your child realize we are part of a community of imperfect people. No one in your family is perfect. No friend is beyond making a mistake. Remind children that they are lovable despite their faults and can love and forgive others as well. It is easier to forgive when we see that everyone makes mistakes.

Model forgiveness. Many parents force forgiveness by requiring an "I'm sorry" or "I forgive you" in the midst of sibling arguments and playdate fights. This simplistic approach won't hold up as relationships become more complicated. Be intentional about modeling true apologies and forgiveness. If your children have witnessed an argument, let them also witness the reconciliation whenever possible. You might try recreating your apologies in your child's presence after arguments have been settled privately.

For additional tips and reference information, visit **www.mvpkids.com**.

Teach the skill of apology. As soon as your child is old enough to speak, stop apologizing for him or her and let your child offer an apology when needed. It's okay to help provide the words, but let your child say it. As your children grow, they may need help with ideas to express a sincere apology. When words aren't enough, help your child make it right. Some ways to show apology are to replace something, give a thoughtful gift, or offer a service. Going beyond words shows extra sincerity and values a relationship.

Teach the cost of holding a grudge. Help children see how holding a grudge hurts them personally. Point out if they are becoming isolated from others or if you notice changes in their personality and behaviors. Did you know that holding a grudge even affects health? Researchers have found that people holding a grudge are likely to get sick more often, stay sick longer, and have greater long-term health complications than those who forgive.

Let them practice. Give older children space to practice problem-solving skills by refusing to be a go-between in their friendships or sibling relationships. Unless children are in an unsafe situation, require that they solve their own squabbles. Offer advice when asked, but give them a chance to mend relationships before stepping in yourself.

Forgiveness is not a free pass. Help children distinguish between mistakes and intentional wrongs. Teach your children that they can forgive without minimizing the situation. Forgiveness does not take away consequences. Peers who regularly act selfishly or make poor choices should not be considered friends. Children should never remain nor put themselves in an unsafe situation. It is possible to forgive without continuing a destructive relationship.

Meet the
mvpkids®
featured in
Liam Conquers Fort Grudge™

LIAM JOHNSON

EZEKIEL JORDAN

OLIVIA WAGNER

LEO RUSSO

FRANKIE RUSSO

Also featuring...

MR. MICHAEL JOHNSON
"Dad"

MRS. DASHA JOHNSON
"Mom"

ESME JOHNSON
Sister

AVA JOHNSON
Sister

Grow up with our mvpkids®

Ages 0-6   **Ages 4-8**

Our **Celebrate!™** series in board book and paperback focus on social and emotional learning. Helpful Teaching Tips are included in each book to equip mentors and parents. Also available are expertly written, related SEL curriculum and interactive Google and Android downloadable apps.

Ages 4-8

Our **Mighty Tokens™** paperback series helps emerging readers learn positive concepts with an experienced reader. Parents or mentors read one side of the page and children read the other side. Each book deposits tokens of affirmation into children so that they may someday become mighty adults.

Early Elementary
Ages 4-10

Our **Help Me Become™** series for early elementary readers tells three short stories in each book of our MVP Kids® inspiring character growth. Each story concludes with a discussion guide to help the child process the story and apply the concepts.

Ages 8 and up

Step back in time with **DNA Chronicles™**, our historical fiction adventure series. Our MVP Kids® weave the past and the present, reliving actual historical events, to experience the history and culture of their ancestors. In these chapter books, readers will learn about the character and fortitude it takes to commit to life's most important values, life skills, and accomplishments.

Elementary

Ages 6-12

Help your children grow in understanding emotions by collecting the entire **Help Me Understand™** series!

*Our **Help Me Understand™** series for elementary readers shares the stories of our MVP Kids® learning to understand and manage specific emotions. Readers will gain tools to take responsibility for their own emotions and develop healthy relationships.*

Lucas Tames the Anger Dragon — SOPHIA DAY

Miriam Lassoes the Worry Whirlwind — SOPHIA DAY

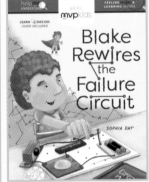
Blake Rewires the Failure Circuit — SOPHIA DAY

Olivia Uproots the Arrogant Weed — SOPHIA DAY

Yong Breaks Out of the Boredom Box — SOPHIA DAY

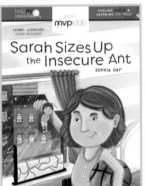
Sarah Sizes Up the Insecure Ant — SOPHIA DAY

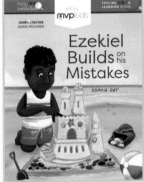
Ezekiel Builds on his Mistakes — SOPHIA DAY

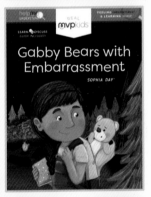
Gabby Bears with Embarrassment — SOPHIA DAY

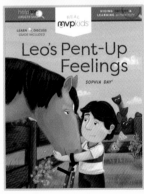
Leo's Pent-Up Feelings — SOPHIA DAY

Annie's Jar of Patience — SOPHIA DAY

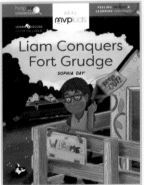
Liam Conquers Fort Grudge — SOPHIA DAY

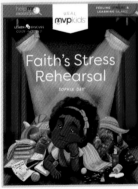
Faith's Stress Rehearsal — SOPHIA DAY

www.mvpkids.com

YONG CHEN

LEO RUSSO

FRANKIE RUSSO

JULIA ROJAS

GABBY GONZALEZ

ANNIE JAMES

AANYA PATEL

BLAKE JAMES

SARAH COHEN-GOLDSTEIN